GREAT JOBS

PLUMBER

Katherine Frew

HIGH interest books

Ch...
A Division of Scholastic Inc.
New York/Toronto/London/Auckland/Sydney
Mexico City/New Delhi/Hong Kong
Danbury, Connecticut

Book Design: Christopher Logan and Daniel Hosek
Production: Mindy Liu
Contributing Editor: Geeta Sobha
Photo Credits: Cover © Photodisc/Getty Images; pp. 4, 33, 38 © Royalty-Free/Corbis; p. 7 Maura B. McConnell; p. 8 © Benjamin Rondel/Corbis; p. 11 © Vanni Archive/Corbis; pp. 12, 15 © Hulton/Archive/Getty Images; p. 16 © Jonny Buzzerio/Corbis; p. 19 © Ted Spiegel/Corbis; p. 21 © Jim Craigmyle/Corbis; p. 24 © David Bentley/Corbis; p. 27 © Mikael Karlsson mike@arrestingimages.com; p. 28 © Robert Holmes/Corbis; pp. 31, 37 © Jon Feingersh/Corbis; p. 34 © Roger Ressmeyer/Corbis; p. 41 © Tim Pannell

Library of Congress Cataloging-in-Publication Data

Frew, Katherine.
Plumber / by Katherine Frew.
p. cm.
Summary: Introduces the profession of plumbing, including its history, tools, typical jobs, importance to public health, and areas of specialization.
Includes bibliographical references and index.
ISBN 0-516-24088-9 (lib. bdg.)—ISBN 0-516-25935-0 (pbk.)
1. Plumbing—Juvenile literature. [1. Plumbing—Vocational guidance. 2. Vocational guidance.] I. Title.

TH6124.F76 2003
696'.1'023—dc21

2003010404

Published in 2004 by Children's Press, an imprint of Scholastic Library Publishing.
Published simultaneously in Canada.
Printed in the United States of America.

1 2 3 4 5 6 7 8 9 10 R 13 12 11 10 09 08 07 06 05 04

Contents

RELIEF VALVE

Introduction

You receive an urgent call from someone at the minor league baseball stadium in your town. The final game of the season is tomorrow afternoon. Unfortunately, the hot water heater, or hot water tank (HWT), for the home team's locker room has broken down. Without an HWT, the players won't be able to shower before or after the game or nurse their sore muscles. The stadium needs a plumber—fast.

You load up your van and head for the stadium. As a plumber, you've had years of experience dealing with HWTs. However, each one is a new puzzle to figure out. The problem water heater is in the basement of the stadium. First you turn off the electricity and the water supply for the HWT. Then you take out the plug in the top of the unit. Using your flashlight, you look inside for rust. There is none, so you check the

Plumbers don't just install or fix pipes. They work on many important household appliances, such as hot water heaters.

heating elements next. Electric HWTs have a number of electric coils that are the heating elements. These coils become very hot and heat the surrounding water. You locate the heating elements and start checking each one's electrical output. You eventually find that one of the heating elements has no output at all. It will need to be replaced.

It's a good thing you have your van of supplies with you. After replacing the heating element, you turn on the water. Once the tank fills up, you turn on the electricity. After the water heats up, you turn on a hot water faucet and out flows warm water. You did it! That's one more puzzle solved. You now have a very grateful team of baseball players.

A plumber's workday is filled with challenges, both mental and physical. Plumbers work on systems that carry water, waste, and gas. Being a plumber requires knowledge of many types of appliances and fixtures in order to solve problems quickly. Plumbers also need to know specific local codes and regulations about their job. Plumbers must be able to handle

Plumbers' trucks are like giant toolboxes: They carry all the necessary equipment to fix almost any plumbing problem.

heavy-duty lifting. Also, at times, they have to rip out old pipes or knock down a wall to do their job.

A plumber's customers are always very grateful for a job well done. Without a toilet that will flush or a kitchen sink that will drain properly, our daily lives would be less comfortable. More important, public health could be at risk. If you think you'd like the challenges of keeping a city or town's water flowing, read on to find out more about this exciting profession.

CHAPTER ONE

Aqueducts to Pipes: A History of Plumbing

Modern-day plumbing is essential to maintaining public health, not to mention comfort. Today, we take conveniences such as our sewage systems and indoor plumbing for granted. People did not always get rid of human waste in a safe and clean manner, though. In the past, waste was often just thrown into open ditches. Water became contaminated. Because of this, many people would get sick from drinking dirty water.

Wash It All Away

The ancient Romans had a special way of keeping their cities clean. They built a sewer system to get rid of human waste. The project started in 735 B.C. It took 225 years to finish. Today, parts of Rome's sewer system are *still* being used.

Ancient Roman baths were spa-like places where people could meet daily. The Romans built baths in many of the places they conquered. This one is in Bath, England.

Ancient Romans also built aqueducts to bring fresh water into the city. Aqueducts are man-made waterways that bring water from a faraway spring or river. Rome's aqueducts took water from sources such as underground springs and brought it to public fountains. Only the homes of the very rich had water brought directly by pipes linked to the aqueducts. Modern-day aqueducts use powerful pumps to transport water where it is needed.

In the nineteenth century, a sewage system using underground rivers was invented in Europe. This new system kept the cities and the drinking water clean by carrying waste away from cities. When cities were built in the United States, people used lessons learned from European sewer systems. They built homes near running water so that waste could be carried off by the water. Also, they made improvements to sewer systems. For example, Washington, D.C., was the first U.S. city to have a sewer built with concrete. Concrete was stronger than the clay, brick, and logs that were used previously.

The water in ancient Rome's aqueducts had to be kept at a certain height to keep it running to the city. High archways like the one shown here supported the aqueduct system.

Pipe Dreams

In England, indoor toilets were invented as early as the sixteenth century. In 1596, Sir John Harrington built a toilet for Queen Elizabeth I. However, no one had a toilet except the inventor and the queen. In 1885, Thomas Twyford designed the toilet after which modern toilets are designed—it both flushed and had a ceramic bowl.

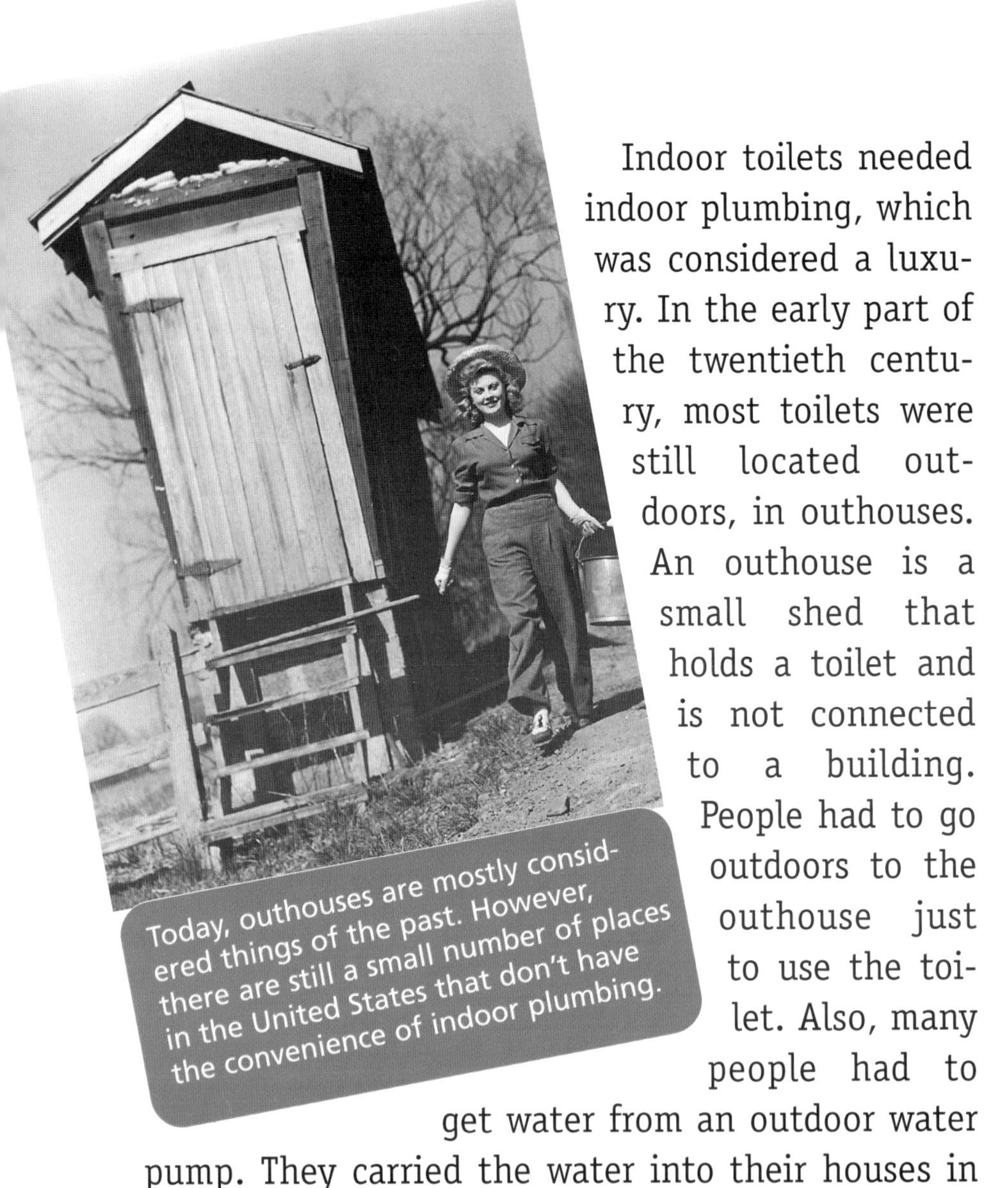
Today, outhouses are mostly considered things of the past. However, there are still a small number of places in the United States that don't have the convenience of indoor plumbing.

Indoor toilets needed indoor plumbing, which was considered a luxury. In the early part of the twentieth century, most toilets were still located outdoors, in outhouses. An outhouse is a small shed that holds a toilet and is not connected to a building. People had to go outdoors to the outhouse just to use the toilet. Also, many people had to get water from an outdoor water pump. They carried the water into their houses in order to cook. After dinner, they had to do their dishes outside!

A system of pipes and fixtures was created to bring drinkable water into buildings and take waste from toilets out of buildings. This is plumbing as we know it today. People can turn on a tap and fill their tub. They can pour themselves a glass of clean water. They can be sure that using their toilet means that their home, and the rest of the town, is being kept clean.

TAKING CARE OF BUSINESS

Thomas Crapper (1836–1910) did not actually invent the toilet, as many people believe. However, Crapper was a successful plumber. He held nine patents for improvements to drains, manhole covers, and other plumbing devices. All of his toilets had the company name, T. Crapper-Chelsea, on them. Because of this, people thought he was responsible for inventing the toilet, too.

PLUMBING IN THE WHITE HOUSE

The first president to live in the White House was John Adams. President Adams moved there in November 1800 with his wife Abigail. At the time, the house was still being built and there was no indoor plumbing. Servants had to carry water from a spring five blocks away!

Things improved in 1833 under President Andrew Jackson. He had indoor plumbing installed in the White House. The huge project involved digging three reservoirs. Underground pipes fed water from the reservoirs into the house. Servants would pump the water from the reservoirs. The water would fill the pipes and the pressure caused by the pumping made the water go to the different floors in the house.

Modern plumbing was finally installed in the White House between 1948 and 1952, during President Harry Truman's term. Plumbers used high-quality materials. They used red brass pipes for the hot and cold water.

Since President Truman's time, plumbing in the White House has undergone many changes. Today, the White House has thirty-five bathrooms and one swimming pool!

Brass and copper tubes were used for the heating, vent, and waste pipes. Toilets as well as new showers and tubs were installed.

When the work was completed, a reporter from *The Plumbing News* magazine wrote, "If they offered me any room in the [White] House, I'd take Mr. Truman's bathroom....Our president's tub is a good 7 feet long—the kind in which a man can stretch out when he comes home from the office....On the opposite wall is the widest washbasin I ever saw. My four kids could all wash their hands there and never rub elbows."

After nearly 150 years, the White House finally had plumbing worthy of the first family!

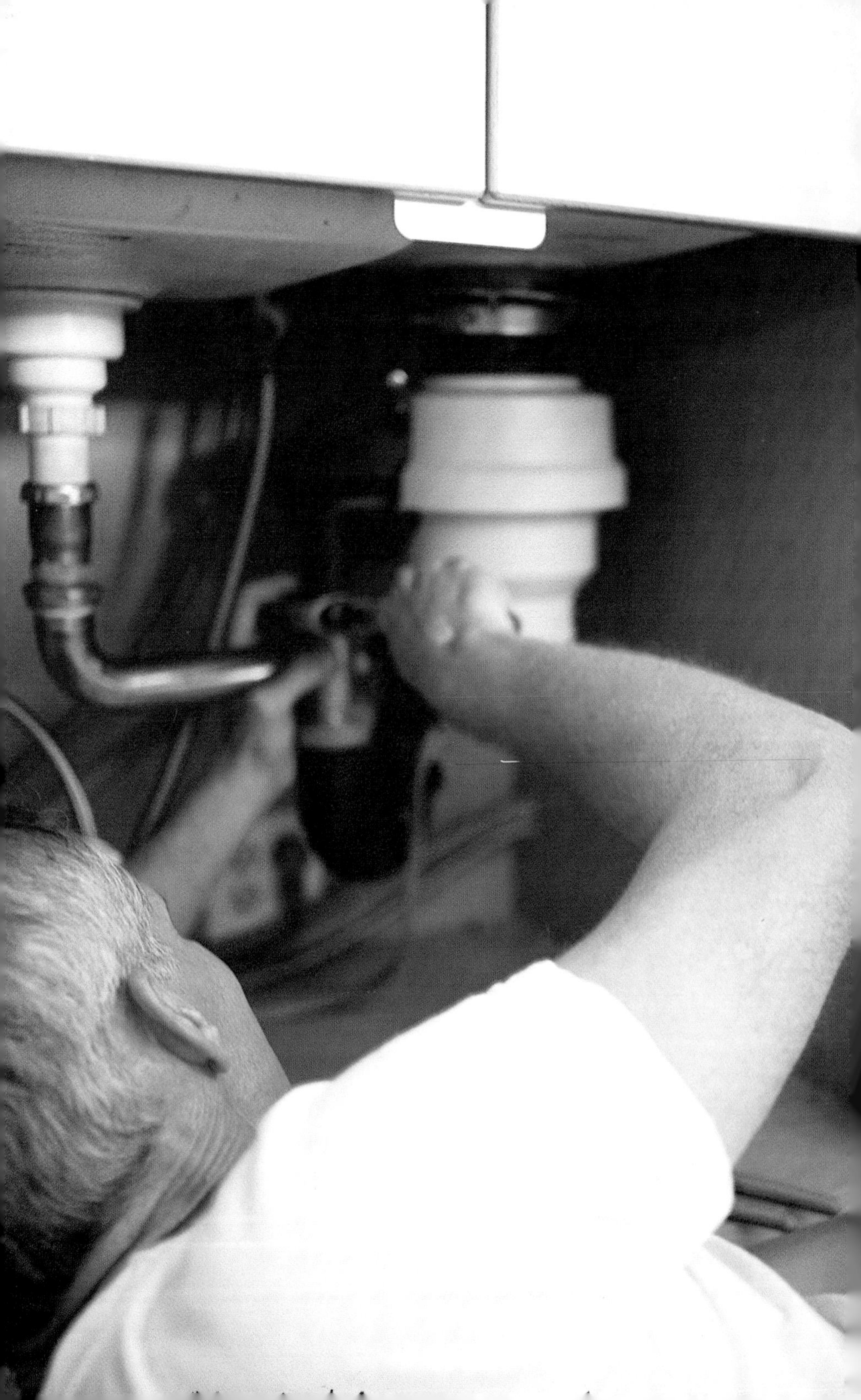

CHAPTER TWO

Becoming a Plumber

There's no doubt about it: The world needs plumbers. If you think plumbing is the job for you, you'll have to learn the tricks of the trade. Plumbing is a business that requires lots of experience. To learn, you can become an apprentice. An apprentice is someone who learns a job by working with a professional who already does that job well—in this case, a master plumber. Apprentice plumbers work with a certified master plumber. They learn all about plumber's tools. They also learn the secrets of doing top-notch work.

Piping Up

Modern-day piping systems need modern-day plumbers. Plumbers are always needed by homeowners and businesses. There's a need for plumbers 24 hours a day, seven days a week. There's rarely a time

Master plumbers have years of experience that help them deal with a variety of problems. They never know if a simple clog will turn out to be an indication of a larger problem.

Some plumbers work with large industrial pipes. The pipe shown here is part of a highway underpass pipe.

when they aren't busy! Most plumbers handle a wide variety of tasks. A plumber might be asked to install appliances, such as washing machines or dishwashers. He or she should also be able to work on a hot water heater or an air-conditioning system.

To be a plumber, you need to be physically strong. Plumbers have to lift heavy equipment. Also, you must enjoy working in many different kinds of settings. Some plumbers choose to work only in homes or offices. Plumbers travel to many different locations for their jobs. Some jobs will take you outside where you'll be exposed to the weather. For example, as a plumber, you may be called to work on a septic tank or a well. A septic tank is an outdoor waste system into which waste from a home goes. However, most jobs take place indoors.

To be a plumber, you need to be good with your hands. Maybe you already like taking things apart and putting them back together. Plumbers use those skills when they install or repair pipes.

You must also be able to think quickly and like solving problems. Imagine that you arrive on a job and the kitchen sink is overflowing. You'll need to

think pretty quickly to keep your client from a water-damage disaster. Organizational skills are also very important. For example, plumbers design the piping plan for a new house. The planner needs to lay the pipes out so that any other plumber who works on them in the future will be able to do his or her job properly.

You should also be able to work well with people. Plumbers sometimes work together. They also work often with construction contractors and homeowners. Finally, a good plumber likes challenges. Every job is a problem for which you must find the solution. Master plumbers with years of experience still enjoy figuring out how to fix a leaking tub or a rattling pipe.

Apprentice to a Master

Apprenticeships usually take four to five years. During that time, apprentices work alongside their teachers. They can choose to apprentice for just one plumber, or they may want to work with a large company. Some large plumbing companies hire apprentices who get to work with many different plumbing professionals.

Some community colleges offer pre-apprentice training. These training courses introduce students to basic plumbing skills and tools. Students also get a chance to meet with and choose a good company for apprenticeship. Choosing a company with a good reputation and a variety of work is important. This work experience is the key to an apprentice's education. He or she will want to get the best learning opportunities possible. Almost all apprenticeship and pre-apprenticeship programs require a high school diploma. It is also suggested that students take as many math classes as possible because plumbers need to be quick with numbers.

It's important for an apprentice to train with a master plumber who can show the right way to handle plumbing problems.

For example, suppose there's a pipe that needs to be cut. A plumber would have to take measurements carefully in order to make sure the pipe is cut to the right size.

Apprentices earn money while learning their skills. However, they only earn about half of what professionals make. They often work during the day and take classes at night. These classes teach plumbing skills, how to use equipment, and important business skills.

Certification

Once the apprenticeship is complete, the student becomes a journeyman plumber. Newly trained plumbers can get certified by their county. This usually involves a small fee and taking a test. While trade certification is not necessary to all areas of plumbing, certain jobs or employers might require it. By getting certified, plumbers prove they are qualified for any sort of job. Certification means that the plumber is aware of all the plumbing codes of the area in which he or she is working. In southern California, for example, plumbers need to know all the codes regarding earthquake faults.

Tools of the Trade

A plumber works with a wide assortment of basic tools. The adjustable wrench has jaws for gripping pipes. Plumbers use a basin wrench to tighten nuts in small spaces. They also use a tube cutter to cut copper tubes. Hacksaws have a jagged blade for cutting metal pipes. A propane torch uses propane gas to produce a flame. It is used for joining pipes together. A plumber's snake is a long wire or coil that is used for cleaning drains.

As the plumber gains experience, he or she will learn how to use a wider variety of tools. Each plumber's toolbox will differ from another, especially for those who specialize in certain areas of plumbing.

High-tech Plumbing

Plumbers today use high-tech equipment to do their work. One important tool is the sewer camera. This tool is used for looking into clogged drains and sewers. The camera is fitted to a sewer cable. The plumber lowers it into the pipe or the sewer. The camera lets the plumber and his or her client see exactly what the problem is. There is a receiver that lets the operator know exactly how deep and where in the sewer the camera is.

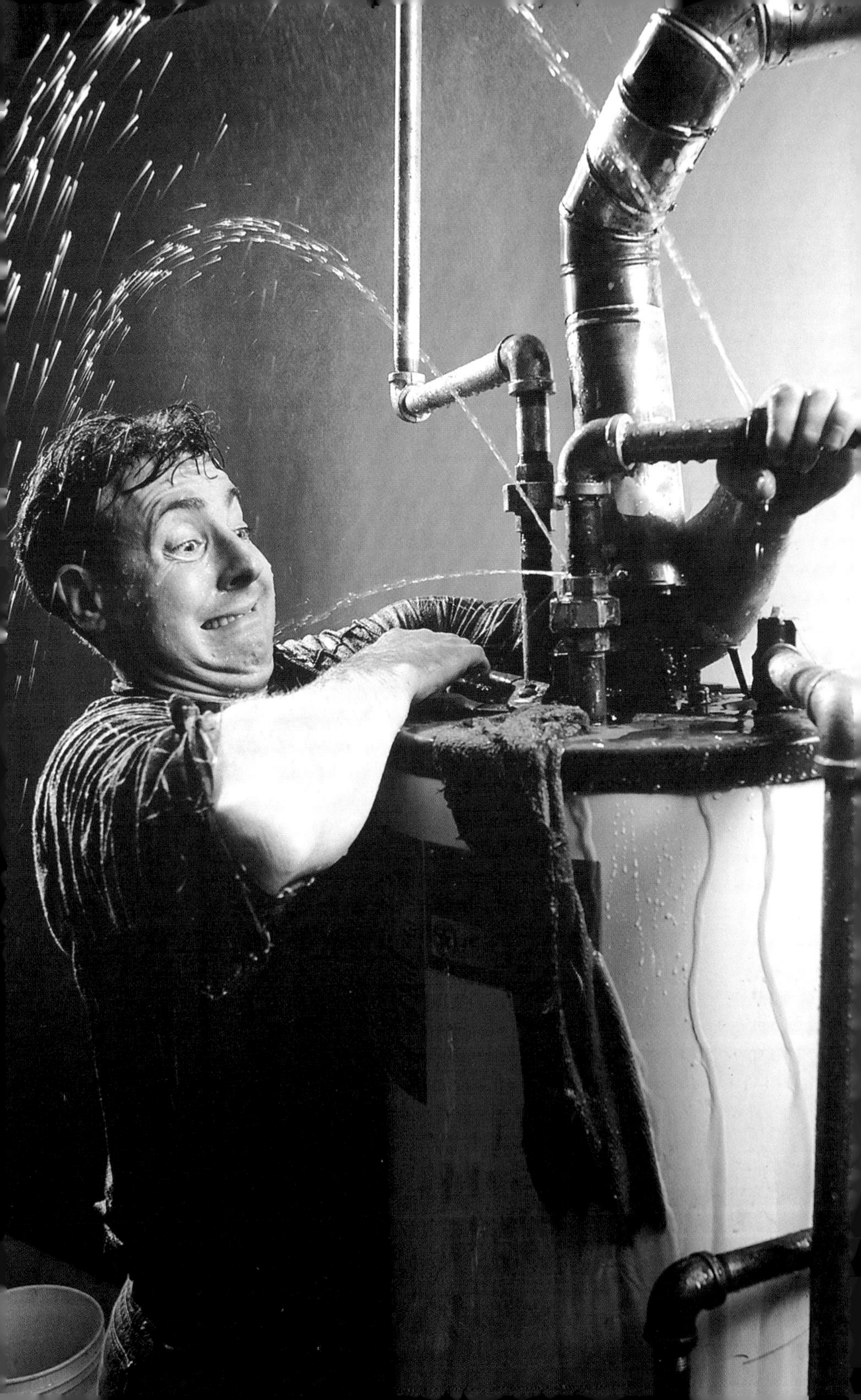

CHAPTER THREE

A Plumber's Day

Plumbing is an exciting profession that is full of challenges and satisfaction. Let's take a look at Josh's day on the job as an apprentice plumber.

8:30 A.M.

I arrive at the office where we keep our two vans and all the equipment the plumbers at Lloyd & Sons use. I've been an apprentice at Lloyd & Sons for two years now. It's been hard work, but I've gained a lot of knowledge. Still, I know there's a lot more for me to learn.

Fred and Jennifer are already at the office. Fred Lloyd owns the business and Jennifer is one of the three professional plumbers he employs. They are my supervisors. Although I've been working as an apprentice plumber for two years, I'm not licensed

Unlike this homeowner with no knowledge of plumbing, professional plumbers need not worry about springing a leak: They're trained to come to the rescue of *any* plumbing problem!

to work without a master plumber present. We often work as teams and solve problems together.

This morning, we're driving out to a job site where a new house is being built. We've already been out there two times. On the first trip, we met our client Bill, a contractor from Breeson Construction. A contractor follows an architect's plans, which show how a new house is to be built. We spoke to Bill about what the family wanted in their new home. It's important to know how many people are going to be living there and how large a family might grow. It's also important to know how much money a client wants to spend. This helps us know what kinds of fixtures and appliances to recommend to them.

Making Plans

We studied the plans of the house and decided where the pipes would need to lay. Then we drew our own design for the pipes. We had to consider which areas of the house would use the most water. We also had

Plumbers have to make sure that pipes are well connected during construction of a home. Even minor mistakes can eventually lead to major problems for homeowners.

to make sure the pipes we used were the right sizes for the various functions they would handle.

House Call

Within a few weeks, the house was under construction. Bill called to tell us it was time to lay the pipes. It was hard work. Jennifer, Fred, and I worked closely with the construction crew. We had to make sure that the pipes fit between the floors and between the walls. I used a wrench to screw the pipes tightly together. I also used a propane torch and solder to add extra sections onto the main pipe. Solder is pieces of metal that can be melted to join pipes together.

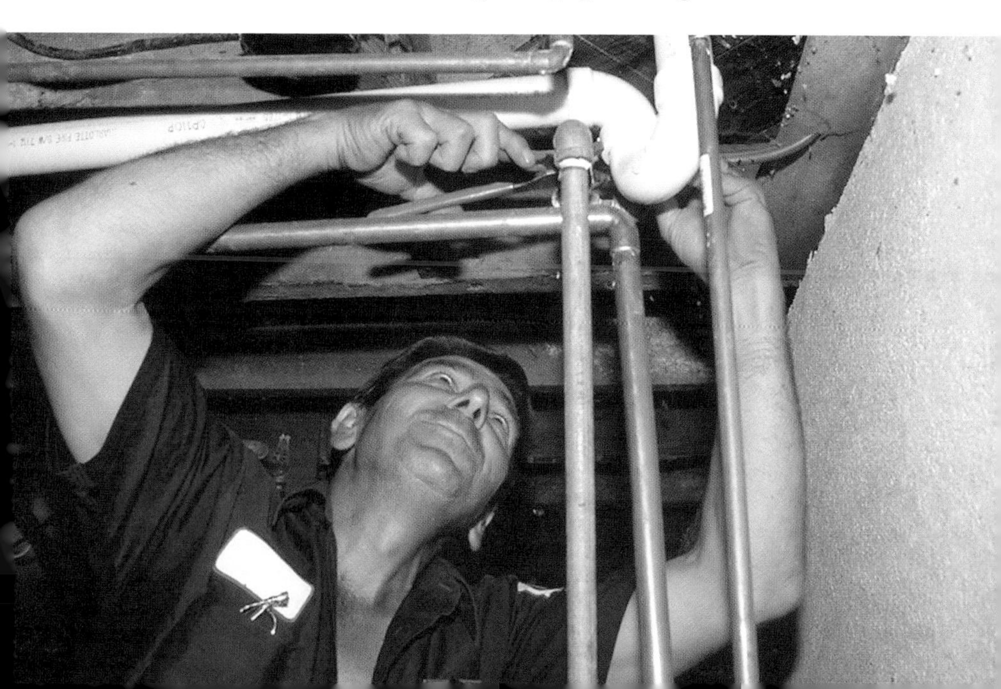

Once all the pipes were cut and measured and all the pieces were clamped together, we tested each section for leaks. Everything had to be perfect because when we are finished, the walls will be sealed up. We don't want a leak to spring and have to tear down an entire wall!

This morning, we're making our final trip. We've got a big day ahead of us.

9:00 A.M.

Bill is at the job site to meet us. He and Fred plan the day's work while Jennifer and I go to inspect the fixtures that have arrived. After the inspection, Jennifer and I start on the bathroom that's connected to the master bedroom. We install a very large bathtub. It weighs a couple of hundred pounds. We move the tub into place. Then we fit the pipes onto the tub. Next, we seal the edges around the drain and the wall with plumber's putty.

Just as we're finishing the bathtub, Jennifer's pager begins to beep. "That's Scott at the office,"

Plumbers must always keep up with popular trends, such as hot tubs, in order to keep up with the competition.

she says. Scott is Fred's son. He works in the office to keep the business running smoothly. Jennifer calls him right away. After she speaks with Scott, Jennifer tells us that there's an emergency at the Johnsons' house. "There seems to be a leak in the basement," Jennifer says.

"You'd better go over there and check it out. Josh and I will finish this job," Fred says to Jennifer. "Call us if you need a hand."

Jennifer leaves to help the Johnsons. I've seen a lot of emergencies come up since I started as an apprentice. We're always there to help out whomever needs us.

3:00 P.M.

We've finally finished installing all the fixtures in the house. Each bathtub and sink had to be connected to pipes. They were then sealed and tested. Now that we've finished, the house is ready to be lived in. Without the running water we just provided, no one could comfortably stay here.

When customers call with a plumbing emergency, plumbers must be ready to take care of the problem. Many plumbers work from an office that can page them to report emergencies.

As Fred and I load up our truck, we talk about our next appointment. We have to repair an air-conditioning system at an office. Just as we're ready to leave, Fred gets a call on his cell phone. It's Jennifer.

"The Johnsons' basement is all right for now," she reports. "The problem is with an old pipe that has rusted through. They have some water damage, but I was able to patch the section that was leaking. We may have to replace the whole pipe, though."

"Great work," Fred says. He then calls Scott at the office to check for any more jobs that may have come up.

As we pull away from the construction site, I look back at the newly built house. I imagine the happy family that will live there. They will cook their dinner, take baths, and wash their clothes. It's great to know my work will help make them comfortable. I'm ready for the next job.

The quality work of experienced plumbers can provide their customers with years of worry-free service.

CHAPTER FOUR

Keeping the Flow Going

Protecting the Public's Health

Being a plumber is one of the most important jobs around. Without pipes, sinks, and toilets that work properly, public health could be at risk. Plumbers keep septic tanks and sewers working so that the water supply is safe and clean. Plumbers live by the motto, "Plumbers protect the health of the nation." They are necessary and valued in every community.

Specialization

Some plumbers decide to specialize in one area. This means that they become experts at one particular job. For example, one plumber might decide to specialize in hot water heaters. Another may decide that installing dishwashers is the way to go.

Sewer cameras are not just used for home inspection. Here, a sewer camera is being used to check for cracks in a sewer after an earthquake in California.

In smaller communities, general plumbers are very important. They are also important on construction sites. Contractors prefer to deal with one excellent journeyman plumber who can handle work in many areas.

Your Own Boss

One of the best parts of being a plumber is having the choice of working in a company or working for yourself. During apprenticeship, larger companies offer a variety of work and great experience. Once you are a journeyman plumber at a company, you don't have to deal with the tasks of running your own business. Also, a large company is less likely to go out of business and leave you without a job.

Being your own boss has its own advantages, though. There's a lot of flexibility and satisfaction in running everything by yourself or with a partner. You can set your own schedule and choose your clients. Owning and running your own business also involves a lot of responsibility. All of the office work of a company, such as contracts, must be

Having good social skills is important to being a good plumber. Plumbers often have to explain the work they do to their customers.

taken care of. Also, there's not a lot of job security—if you can't get enough jobs, you could lose money and maybe go out of business.

In between these two options are companies like Roto-Rooter. If a plumber decided to join Roto-Rooter, he or she receives all the elements needed to run a business. Telephones and computers, business training, Roto-Rooter uniforms, and adver-

tising are all provided. There is also the security of having a well-known name and a large company supporting your new business. In exchange for all of this, Roto-Rooter receives a percentage of your income. You are also required to use their company name and logo on all of your jobs.

Plumbing With Pride

Plumbing is one career that will always provide challenges. As technology moves ahead, so does the plumbing industry. Today, plumbers work with high-tech appliances and fixtures such as whirlpool baths and electronic faucets. Protecting the environment has become very important. Those in the plumbing industry must keep up with the environmental laws. For example, those who work with air conditioners must know how to handle chlorofluorocarbons (CFCs) that are used for cooling. CFCs are gases used in air conditioners that can be damaging to the environment.

On large air-conditioning units, plumbers install piping that runs through the building.

Nearly every person in the world comes in contact with the work of plumbers. Those who choose to become plumbers know how important their job is. Whether a pipe bursts or a drain clogs, a plumber is the person to call. This profession is one that will always be in demand.

TAKING CARE OF BUSINESS

Some plumbing companies are even older than the United States. The Diller Wierman Company was founded in 1765—eleven years before the American colonies declared their independence!

Families everywhere appreciate the conveniences of today's household appliances. Plumbers keep these appliances, such as dishwashers, in working order.

NEW WORDS

appliance (uh-**plye**-uhnss) a machine designed to do a particular job

apprentice (uh-**pren**-tiss) someone who learns a trade or craft by working with a skilled person

aqueduct (**ak**-wuh-duhkt) a large bridge built to carry water across a valley

certification (sur-tif-uh-**kay**-shuhn) when someone is given a piece of paper that officially states that they are qualified to do a job

contractor (kon-**trak**-tur) a person who is hired to build something, such as a house or building

convenience (kuhn-**vee**-nyuhnss) something that is useful and easy to use

faults (**fawlts**) large cracks in the earth's surface that can cause earthquakes

fixtures (**fiks**-churz) things that are fixed firmly and permanently in place, for example a sink tap or showerhead

NEW WORDS

install (in-**stawl**) to put something in place, ready to be used

journeyman plumber (**jur**-nee-man **pluhm**-ur) an experienced and reliable plumber who has finished his or her apprenticeship

patents (**pat**-uhnts) legal documents giving the inventor of some items sole rights to manufacture and sell the items

receiver (ri-**see**-vur) a piece of equipment that receives radio or television signals and changes them into sounds or pictures

reservoir (**rez**-ur-vwar) a natural or artificial holding area for storing a large amount of water

septic tank (**sep**-tik **tangk**) a tank in which the solid sewage is disintegrated by bacteria

sewage (**soo**-ij) liquid and solid waste that is carried away in sewers and drains

specialize (**spesh**-uh-lize) to focus on one area of work

FOR FURTHER READING

Massey, Howard C. *Plumber's Handbook*. Carlsbad, CA: Craftsman Book Company, 1998.

Paige, Joy. *Cool Careers Without College for People Who Love to Build Things*. New York: Rosen Publishing Group, 2002.

Smith, Lee. *Math for Plumbers and Pipefitters*. Stamford, CT: Delmar Learning, 1995.

Web sites

MasterPlumbers.com: Plumbviews
www.masterplumbers.com/plumbviews/2000/education.asp
Check out this Web site for information on education and apprenticeships. You can even have your questions answered by master plumbers on their message board.

theplumber.com
www.theplumber.com
Read about the history of plumbing and find the answers to some frequently asked plumbing questions.

College View — Job Profiles: Plumber
www.collegeview.com/career/careersearch/job_profiles/construct/plu01.html
This Web site describes the plumber's job and its pros and cons. You can find out how to get started on the path to becoming a plumber.

Organizations

United Association of Journeymen
and Apprentices
901 Massachusetts Avenue
NW Washington, DC 20001
www.ua.org

International Association of Plumbing
and Mechanical Officials (IAPMO)
5001 E. Philadelphia St.
Ontario, CA 91761
(909) 472-4100
www.iapmo.org

American Water Works Association
6666 W. Quincy Avenue
Denver, CO 80235
(303) 794-7711
www.awwa.org

INDEX

INDEX

About the Author

Katherine Frew is a writer living in Texas, where she is currently working on her master's degree in English literature.